KETOGENIC
DIET
slow cooker
COOKBOOK

Top 50 Easy and Delicious **Keto Diet Slow Cooker Recipes** for Extreme Weight Loss

Published by The Fruitful Mind

Disclaimer

Table of Contents

4

Introduction

Welcome to the *Ketogenic Diet Slow Cooker Cookbook: Top 50 Easy and Delicious Ketogenic Slow Cooker Recipes for Extreme Weight Loss (Keto and Low Carb)*. I really appreciate your dedication and efforts to download/order this cookbook which is among a series of low carb and Keto cookbooks. This series of cookbooks is aimed at exemplifying the effortless and simple nature of cooking.

Since an ideal body weight and healthier body condition are big concerns nowadays, diet has become the trend among modern communities. Many people (and maybe you) have tried a lot of dieting methods alongside all of the hard treatments around. Some have gone to the extent of paying expensively to attain the ideal body weight they desire.

It has been seen in the current setting that many dieting methods are popping up. Surely, all of them offer the fastest way to lose weight. Complete with some wonderful programs, all of these dieting methods seem too good to be ignored. Once a dieting method is promoted via the television show, some people will always rush to give it a try.

Furthermore, they are more than willing to change from one dieting method to another dieting method.

The fact is that no matter how hard people have tried, it seems that there is little or no progress at all. Some people may lose pounds of weight and gain many kilos in a short period. How can this happen? Surely, many of the dieting methods do work. However, everyone has a different physical makeup. This is why a method that is good for one person may not be effective for another person. It is important to know which dieting method suits your body to be able to effectively reach your ideal body weight without wasting your time.

You might have heard that the ketogenic diet is a dieting method that has been effective for the last several years. It is often known as a low carb diet. Principally, ketogenic diet involves high intake of fat, moderate consumption of protein, and tremendously low consumption of carbohydrates. In other words, the ketogenic diet can be said to be a dieting method that encourages the liver to produce more ketones.

After the mealtime, it is a norm that your body will change the carbs you consume into glucose. Glucose is chosen as the main energy source since it is the easiest molecule in the human body to convert. As glucose fulfills the need of energy for the body, the fats stay and are heaped up in your body leading to weight gain.

When you revert to this ketogenic dieting method, the number of carb intake is tightly limited and the body will reach a condition called ketosis—a condition where the body tries to survive when the food intake is low. As a response to this condition, the liver will change fats into ketones that will be used as the energy resource. By doing this, the amount of fats in the body will reduce so you will reach your ideal body weight and feel more healthy and energized.

You will enjoy an ideal body weight and a healthier body that is strong and not easily attacked by dangerous diseases such as type 2-diabetes, high cholesterol level, etc. Another interesting advantage of following a ketogenic diet is that you will feel lightweight and be more energetic. Read on to enjoy the great recipes outlined in this book and good luck on your journey!

Facts about the Ketogenic Diet

The general definition of the word "Keto" is derived from a bodily metabolic process known as "Ketosis." This process is what allows the body to lose weight so fast while under a Ketogenic Diet.

What is Ketosis? It is the process through which the body releases chemicals called ketones which significantly help to lower down the level of fats in our body.

I will tell you how that works in just a bit.

But, let's get back to Ketogenic Diet first.

So, the primary aim of the Ketogenic Diet is to basically decrease your carbohydrate input to a very basal and minimal level, while at the same time doubling on your fat intake.

And this is precisely why the Ketogenic Diet has also been known as a High-Fat-Low-carb Diet all around the world.

However, before fully explaining how a Ketogenic Diet works you need to learn to appreciate how the body controls its glucose and insulin levels.

To make things clear and easy, whenever our body is taking up a significant amount of carbohydrates, the production or glucose and insulin start to rise as well.

One thing you should know, though, is that glucose is a pretty flexible convertible molecule, which the body uses whenever energy is required.

Alternatively, insulin works as a means of countermeasure if the level of glucose in the bloodstream goes beyond normal levels. If the degree of glucose in the blood is low, insulin levels lower down. On the other hand, if the glucose level rises, insulin helps to lower it down.

You might be wondering now, what does all of this have to do with losing your weight?

Well, whenever your body has a constant supply of glucose, it starts to break it down rather than the fat to get the energy. So, burning down fat is entirely avoided here.

Even if you end up running all day and are in need of an energy boost, the fat just stays there in your body instead as the glucose is being burned for the energy, causing the fat to keep accumulating.

As long as you are on a high carbohydrate diet, the fat levels won't come down because the body is always breaking down carbohydrates.

And this is where Ketogenic Diet kicks in!

Whenever your body is deprived of carbohydrates, it throws the body into a state of "Ketosis" where it will release the aforementioned chemicals called "Ketones."

Ketones then greatly help to encourage the burning down of fat from our bodies.

Eating a ketogenic diet, will help you to lose weight, and put you at less risk of disease. Research has shown that a ketogenic diet can be more effective than 'low-fat' diets. This type of diet enables you to consume nutritious food, that keeps you full for longer, so you don't experience many of the hunger-pang symptoms often associated with other diets. People have been found to lose more than double the amount of weight on a ketogenic diet, compared to low-fat diets. A ketogenic diet will give you more ketones, will lower your blood sugar and improve how your body responds to insulin.

Everyone's body produces molecules known as 'ketones'. When your body is low in blood sugar, these ketones act as fuel for the body. Your body produces more ketones when you reduce how many carbohydrates you eat, and when you restrict the amount of protein you consume. This is because carbohydrates are very quickly broken down into blood sugar; and if you eat too much protein, this too turns into blood sugar.

Your body can also enter ketosis if you were to fast, and not eat anything; your body would naturally start to burn off fat. But, clearly this would be an unhealthy way to reach ketosis. You'd probably feel quite light-headed, hungry, bad tempered and lacking in energy if you were to starve yourself. So, that is not recommended!

Instead, we recommend a ketogenic diet, whereby you eat food that will put you into a ketogenic state, but without the need to fast.

Good Advice for a Ketogenic Diet

1. Drink Plenty of Water

This is good advice for any diet, but it's sensible to ensure you're well hydrated. This means that your body works at its best. Try drinking 3 litres of water a day, this is an ideal amount. It will help you to lose weight, your skin to be hydrated and youthful looking, and your body's organs will work to flush out any toxins. The more water you drink, the easier you'll find to do that each day. Whilst at first, you may need to make more frequent trips to the washroom, this will decrease as more days go by and your body adjusts to it.

2. Intermittent Fasting

Some people on a ketogenic diet also find that fasting is beneficial. This can help you achieve the state of ketosis, because you won't be consuming calories, in terms of protein or carbohydrates. It can be sensible to do a low-carbohydrate diet for a few days before embarking on fasting, but many people find this beneficial. There's a lot of discussion on diets that involve eating for 5 days, and fasting (where you only consume 600 calories per day) for two days. People lose a lot of weight on this technique, and it's also supposed to improve your memory and clarity of thought, and to stave off later life diseases such as dementia and Alzheimer's. Some people, rather than doing the 5 day eating and 2 day fasting, decide to fast a bit each day, and try to extend the time that they fast, so that once they've gone to bed, they then don't eat breakfast, but instead wait and have a late lunch, so to extend their fast. It is important to be well hydrated when you're fasting, so keep drinking, ideally water, but other drinks (provided they're not sugary soft drinks) are fine too.

3. Eat Healthy Salt

Healthy salt almost seems like an oxymoron, a contradiction in terms; as we're told by society that a lot of our food has salt already in it, and not to add it to food. When we eat a lot of carbohydrates, we also tend to have more insulin. But, when we cut out carbohydrates in our diets, we have less insulin, our kidneys get rid of a lot of sodium, which is why it's important for us to consume healthy salt, on a low carbohydrate diet, such as the ketogenic diet. A good healthy salt, of which you can add 3-5g per day to your diet, is pink Himalayan rock salt (this is approximately a tea-spoon throughout the course of a day, you could put a sprinkling here and there on your food). Other ways that you can get healthy salt into your system, is by consuming organic broth. You can also add ¼ teaspoon to 16oz of water and drink that throughout the day. You can eat cucumber and celery which have natural sodium in them, and are also low in carbohydrates. Celery in particular is very good, as you burn more calories chewing and eating it, also digesting it because of the fiber it contains. You can also eat salty sea vegetables such as kelp and nori dishes and this will also increase the good salt you have; finally, there are certain snacks you can eat, such as salted macadamia nuts and salted pumpkin seeds which are delicious as a snack, but will also add a good amount of 'healthy' salt to your diet.

There is a huge difference between what we know as the white common table salt and the pink Himalayan salt. Table salt has been heated to over 1,200 degrees Fahrenheit to allegedly 'purify' it. This type of salt is 97.5% sodium chloride, and contains 2.5% of additives. Because of this process, this destroys all of the natural minerals and goodness that salt contains. There are additives in table salt, which prevent it from clumping together. Table salt can often contain iodine, or fluoride. Whereas, pink Himalayan salt, contains 84 essential minerals that the body needs. It is 85% sodium chloride and 15% minerals. It's a really good source of magnesium, and research has shown that at least 80% of people are deficient in magnesium. Himalayan pink salt, helps the blood sugar in your body to remain at a good level, and finally it helps you to have a good night's sleep, which always makes you feel much better, rejuvenated and ready to take on the world.

4. Exercise

When you're on a Ketogenic diet, it's crucial that you're also participating in high-intensity exercise. By doing this you'll help your body transport those glucose molecules in your blood into your liver and muscles. The more exercise you do, the more easily this process occurs. When you achieve ketosis maintaining a good exercise regime is important, because with time you'll be able to adapt to allowing some more carbohydrates in your diet. The type of exercises that are particularly effective for this type of diet includes: squats, push-ups, pull ups and pull-downs and bent over rows. Many people have found that cross-fit is a particularly good exercise regime or something like circuit training. If you have lots of resistance training exercises, which include sprint running, and walking this will help you to maintain ketosis. Your exercise needn't be excessive. You could do resistance training for 20 minutes 2 days, then spend a day doing more relaxed walking; do another 2 days of resistance training, and again spend a day doing something less energetic, but still getting exercise.

5. Maintain a healthy digestive system

Sometimes people on a Ketogenic diet can find that they suffer from constipation. There are many reasons why this could occur. It could be that the individual has some issues in their gut and can have too much bad bacteria there, or candida. It could be that they're not consuming enough fiber, in the way of vegetables, food and drink. I can't stress enough how important it is to try to drink around 3 litres of water a day (please see point 1 above). Your urine should be clear and not dark yellow. If your urine is dark yellow, then that's a key sign you're dehydrated. A further reason for constipation is that you don't have enough electrolytes in your body, minerals, such as sodium, magnesium, calcium and potassium – this is why eating pink Himalayan rock salt can be a good idea (please see point 3 above).

If you are chronically stressed, this is another factor that can stop your intestines contracting as they should, and moving faeces along your gut. There are things you can do to prevent constipation on a Ketogenic diet, and this includes consuming products that contain good bacteria, such as probiotic yogurts, you can take acidophilus tablets from a health-food shop, each fermented foods, such as sauerkraut, and coconut water. Drink lots of water, and add in Himalayan salt (just a quarter of a teaspoon) into this. If you can drink a 'green' drink a day, such as a smoothie containing apple, spinach, kiwi and kale, this will put more amazing minerals in your body, such as potassium, magnesium and calcium and help your digestive system greatly.

6. Monitor your protein consumption

You need to be eating the right amount of protein for your body. If you eat an excessive amount, then your body will turn it into glucose, which is exactly what we're trying to avoid in the first place. If you're not able to maintain the state of ketosis very well, then it's certainly worth monitoring how much protein you're consuming. People will differ depending on their body type, and how much exercise they do. If you're doing a great deal of resistance training, then you may need more protein than a person who is doing aerobic exercise. As a general rule of thumb, you should be eating 1 gram of protein, for every kilogram that your body weight is. It's good to split this protein up into 2 or 3 servings over the course of the day, and not eat it all at once.

7. Select carbohydrates carefully

A ketogenic diet is by nature, very low in carbohydrates. But, when you do consume carbohydrates, there are certain types that are better for you than others. If you can opt to have non-starchy vegetables and low-glycemic (this means that it will have a minimal effect on how much glucose circulates around your blood); fruit, such as lemons, limes, ½ Granny Smith apple in a green smoothie; or some berries in a protein shake, these are much better for you. When you come out of ketosis, you can add foods like berries, sweet potatoes, grass-fed butter, and cinnamon into your diet. On low carb days, the most you should be putting into smoothies would be ½ a Granny Smith apple, 1 carrot or 1 beetroot. Coconuts are good for you to consume as well, because these contain a good amount of fatty acids.

8. Reduce stress

If you are suffering from chronic stress, you will not be able to achieve a state of ketosis. If something is causing chronic stress in your life, then probably your attention should be focused upon relieving that stress, rather than focusing so much on a Ketogenic diet. This doesn't mean you have to eat a ton of carbohydrates, but you certainly don't need to be so strict or hard on yourself. Just reduce your carbohydrates a bit; sort whatever is stressing you out, and then return to the diet at a later point. When you're in a state of chronic stress, stress hormones will be raised and this in turn raises your blood sugar, so that your adrenaline is high and you're in a state of 'flight or fight'. If your level of stress continues, then your blood sugar increases, and your ketones decrease. My advice would be to work on dealing with whatever is causing the stress; there are some things in life which are out of our control, but we can find the best ways of dealing with issues. Some things take more time than others, but it can vastly reduce stress, to know that you're making progress towards sorting out a problem, even if that progress is slow-going. It can be useful to get a page of A4 paper, and write down one side of it, all the things that are bothering you (issues) and making you feel stressed – try to break these down as much as possible into small chunks. Then write on the right-hand side of the page, how you will resolve these issues (solutions). Most things can be overcome, or at least dealt with in a way that makes it manageable.

Remember that you are a strong person; ensure that you eat as well as you can – if you eat lots of sugary foods, this causes inflammation and makes our bodies weak, eating good food such as avocados, eggs, coconut oil, non-starchy vegetables, grass fed meat, almonds and walnuts, will make you feel better and more able to tackle any issues deftly. Definitely ensure that you drink lots of water, at least 3 litres a day, because this will help you in so many ways, physically and mentally. One really nice technique to give yourself a boost, is to drink lemon water. Lemon naturally gives you energy, it hydrates you, gives you oxygen, so drinking lemon water will make you feel rejuvenated, revitalized and it's very refreshing. Lemon water will boost your immune system, it will also detox your system flushing out any toxins. It will make your skin have less wrinkles and blemishes. Lemon is excellent to get rid of any respiratory complaints. It will help with weight loss. It will help to purify your blood and reduce infection and inflammation. Try to get out for some exercise/fresh-air/and change of scenery whenever you're able, this will help to lift your mood. Be confident that you can find solutions to all of your problems and overcome any hurdles. It can be helpful to read affirmative statements to yourself each day, and this will help you to become more confident. Use the power of visualization to imagine yourself in any situation you wish to be in. There are various herbs you can use that will help to reduce stress too: Panax Ginseng (Asian Ginseng) is used for well-being, and as an anti-depressant. Rhodiola (Golden Root) is used to reduce stress, depression and fatigue. Holy Basil is said to alleviate stress, and also to help with headaches, colds and aid the digestive system. Basil has the most amazing scent, and is so versatile for use in cooking, and smoothies/drinks.

9. Get a good night's sleep

If you aren't sleeping well, then this will have an effect, similar to stress. As a result your blood sugar will rise. Ensure that you go to sleep at a sensible time at night, ideally before 11pm, and ensure that your room is suitably dark, so that you're not disturbed by street lights, or dawn light coming through the windows. It's good to try and get between 7 – 9 hours of sleep per night. If you're stressed, then you need more sleep. Ensure your room is not too hot and stuffy, ideally have a window open slightly to get a little fresh air circulating, or have air conditioning or a fan on. If you're sensitive to light or noise, then consider wearing an eye-mask or ear-plugs so that you're disrupted as little as possible.

Following these 9 points above, can help you achieve and maintain a state of Ketosis. Following the above can also put your body into a state where you burn fat for body fuel and to give you the ability to think clearly and sharply, and can prevent you from craving and consuming carbohydrates, and as a result feeling lethargic and cotton-wool-headed. By following the above 9 points, you'll be giving yourself the best possible head-start for your Ketogenic diet. You'll lose weight and have a leaned and toned physique and lots of energy, so that you'll able to participate fully in all aspects of life.

KETOGENIC
BREAKFAST AND BRUNCH RECIPES

Bacon Mushroom Breakfast

SERVES
4

MINUTES
15

Nutritional info: Cal 166, protein 6.73 g, fat 15.52 g, carbs 2.14 g

Ingredients:
2 cups cooked ground sausage
½ cup chopped onion
1 Tbsp. parsley, dried
1 tsp garlic powder
1 tsp thyme
6 crumbled bacon slices, cooked and drained
2 cups organic chicken broth
1 cup red bell pepper, chopped
½ cup Parmesan cheese
1 cups heavy white cream
2 cups raw mushrooms, sliced
Pepper
Salt

Directions:

Add all the above ingredients to a large slow cooker.

Cook on LOW mode for 4-6 hour. Make sure not to overcook or cook at too high heat or the cream will separate. Serve hot.

Cheesy Spinach Frittata

SERVES
3

MINUTES
15

Nutritional info: Cal 564, protein 32 g, fat 45.3 g, carbs 11.7 g

Ingredients:
1 cup (packed) baby spinach, chopped
1 cup mozzarella cheese (2%), shredded
3 egg whites
3 eggs
1 diced Roma tomato
4 tbsps. olive oil
½ cup diced onion
¼ tsp. black pepper
¼ tsp. white pepper
2 tbsps. milk
Salt

Directions:

In a small skillet, heat the olive oil over medium heat. Add the onion and sauté for about 5 minutes or until tender.

Lightly grease the slow cooker with non-stick cooking spray.

In a large mixing bowl, combine ¾ cup mozzarella cheese, the sautéed onion, and the rest of the ingredients. Transfer to slow cooker.

Sprinkle the remaining ¼ cup of mozzarella cheese over the mixture.

Cover and cook for 1 to 1 1/2 hours on low or until the eggs are set and a knife comes out clean when inserted in the center.

Egg and Sausage Casserole

SERVES
8

MINUTES
20

Nutritional info: Cal 448, protein 26.3 g, fat 36.5 g, carbs 4.3 g

Ingredients:
10 eggs
1 package (12 oz.) sausage, cooked and sliced
¾ cup whipping cream
2 cloves garlic, minced
¼ teaspoon pepper
½ teaspoon salt
½ lb. or 1 medium head broccoli, chopped
1 cup shredded and divided cheddar
3 tablespoon olive oil

Directions:
Grease the slow cooker well with the olive oil.

Layer half of the broccoli, half of the sausages, and then half of the cheese into the greased slow cooker. Repeat the layer with the remaining broccoli, sausages, and cheese.

In a large mixing bowl, whisk the whipping cream, eggs, garlic, salt, and pepper until well mixed. Pour over the layered ingredients in the slow cooker.

Cover and cook for 4-5 hours on low or 2-3 hours on high until the edges are browned and the center is set.

Cheesy Ham Scramble

SERVES
6

MINUTES
10

Nutritional info: Cal 250, protein 15 g, fat 10 g, carbs 3 g

Ingredients:
1 clove garlic, minced
1 teaspoon dried parsley
½ cup cheddar cheese, shredded
½ cup cooked and chopped ham
½ stick butter
½ tsp. oregano
6 large eggs
6 tbsps. coconut or almond milk
Salt
Pepper

Directions:
Heavily grease the slow cooker with the butter, leaving a little to melt in the bottom.

In a mixing bowl, whisk all the ingredients together except for the ham. Stir in the ham and then pour the mixture into the slow cooker. Cook for 2 hours on low, as you stir occasionally.

Egg Chili Puff

SERVES
8

MINUTES
15

Nutritional info: Cal 366, protein 29.9 g, fat 24.8 g, carbs 4.9 g

Ingredients:
16 oz. shredded Monterey Jack cheese
12 eggs
2 cans (4 oz. each) diced green chilies
2 cups creamed cottage cheese
1 tsp. salt
½ tsp. pepper

Directions:
Grease the slow cooker with non-stick cooking spray. Turn the heat to high. While the slow cooker is heating, whisk all of the ingredients together in a mixing bowl.

Slowly pour the whisked ingredients into the slow cooker. Cover with lid. Cook for 2 hours on high. Adjust heat to low and continue cooking for another 3 hours.

Cajun Grits

SERVES
8

MINUTES
5

Nutritional info: Cal 283, protein 11.6 g, fat 23.4 g, carbs 6.8 g

Ingredients:
1½ cups soy grits
12 oz. grated cheddar cheese
2 cups cream
4 tbsps. butter
6 cups water
2 tsps. salt

Directions:
Grease the slow cooker with non-stick cooking spray.

Add the water, salt, and soy grits.

Cook for 7 hours or overnight on low.

Before serving, remove the lid. Add the butter, cream, and the grated cheese.

Serve with additional grated cheese or butter.

Spinach and Sausage Breakfast Frittata

SERVES
6

MINUTES
10

Nutritional info: Cal 238, protein 20 g, fat 16 g, carbs 3 g

Ingredients:
¾ cups frozen spinach, drained and chopped
1 ½ cups diced red bell pepper
¼ cup diced red onion
8 beaten eggs
1 teaspoon sea salt
½ teaspoon black pepper
1 1/3 cups cooked sausage

Directions:
Grease the slow cooker with non-stick cooking spray and mix all the ingredients in it.

Cook for 2-3 hours on low. Serve warm.

Creamy Hot Cocoa

SERVES
4

MINUTES
20

Nutritional info: Cal 40, protein 3 g, fat 5 g, carbs 3 g

Ingredients:
¼ cup and 2 tbsps. unsweetened cocoa powder
2 packets of Stevia
¼ tsp. salt
1 tsp. vanilla
3 cups of unsweetened almond milk
¼ cup of Half and half

Directions:
Combine all the ingredients in a slow cooker.

Cook covered for 2 hours on low, stirring occasionally.

Stir well and serve warm.

Hash Brown Casserole

SERVES
8

MINUTES
10

Nutritional info: Cal 342, protein 21 g, fat 22 g, carbs 14 g

Ingredients:
20 oz. frozen hash browns, shredded
8 slices of thick cut cooked and chopped bacon
8 oz. shredded Cheddar cheese
8 thinly sliced green onions
12 large eggs
½ cup milk
½ teaspoon salt
¼ teaspoon pepper

Directions:
Grease a slow cooker with oil and layer hash browns, bacon, cheese and green onions, repeating the layering another time.

Whisk together the rest of the ingredients and pour over.

Cook for 2-3 hours on high. Serve hot.

Easy Morning Pie

SERVES
6

MINUTES
10

Nutritional info: Cal 449, protein 22.9 g, fat 36.7 g, carbs 7.1 g

Ingredients:
1 lb. pork sausage, broken up
8 eggs, whisked
2 tsps. basil, dried
1 yellow diced onion
1 tbsp. garlic powder
1 shredded sweet potato or yam
4 tbsp. olive oil
1 tbsp. salt
1 tbsp. pepper
Vegetables of your choice (squash, peppers, etc.)

Directions:
Grease the slow cooker with the olive oil.

Put all of the ingredients into the slow cooker and mix well.

Cook for 6-8 hour on low or until the pork sausage is cooked through. Slice into 6-8 pie slices.

KETOGENIC
STEWS AND CHILIS

Chili Leeks Steak

SERVES
12

MINUTES
15

Nutritional info: Cal 540, protein 32.47 g, fat 31 g, carbs 5.67 g

Ingredients:
2½ pounds grass fed steak, cubed
1 tbsp. Ancho chili powder
½ tsp. ground cumin
½ tsp. salt
1/8 tsp. ground black pepper
¼ tsp. ground cayenne pepper
½ cup of sliced Leeks
2 cups canned tomatoes, whole with juice
1 cup of chicken stock

Toppings:
2 tbsps. Sour cream
¼ cup of shredded Cheddar cheese
½ sliced Avocado
1 tsp. Fresh and chopped cilantro

Directions:

Combine all the above ingredients in the slow cooker except the toppings. Stir the ingredients well.

Cook for approximately 6 hours on high. Top with the toppings and serve warm.

Chicken & Mushroom Soup

SERVES
6

MINUTES
20

Nutritional info: Cal 455, protein 34.5 g, fat 32.4 g, carbs 5.2 g

Ingredients:
3 tbsps. unsalted butter, melted and divided
3 cups homemade chicken broth, divided
¾ cup fresh and sliced mushrooms
2 celery chopped stalks
1 large chopped onion
1 chopped scallion
3 garlic minced cloves
½ lb. bacon
4 (4 oz.) skinless, boneless grass-fed chicken breasts
1 cup heavy cream
1 teaspoon dried and crushed oregano
Sea salt
Freshly ground black pepper
¼ cup fresh chopped cilantro

Directions:

In a slow cooker, mix together 2 tablespoons of butter, one cup of broth and vegetables.

Set the slow cooker on Low. Cover and cook for about 1 hour.

Meanwhile, heat a large skillet on medium-high heat. Add bacon and cook for about 4-5 minutes. Transfer bacon onto a paper towel-lined plate to drain.

In the same skillet, melt the remaining butter on medium-high heat.

Add chicken and cook for 4-5 minutes per side. Remove from heat and keep aside to cool. Now cut chicken into bite-sized pieces.

After 1 hour of cooking, add chicken, bacon, remaining broth, cream, oregano, salt and black pepper to slow cooker and stir well.

Set the slow cooker on Low. Cover and cook for about 6-8 hours.

Transfer the chicken into a bowl, and with 2 forks, shred the chicken breasts. Return the chicken to the soup and stir to mix.

Serve this with the garnishing of fresh cilantro.

Chicken & Kale Soup

SERVES
6

MINUTES
15

Nutritional info: Cal 268, protein 34.9 g, fat 8.1 g, carbs 12.8 g

Ingredients:
2 tbsps. unsalted butter, melted
4 cups cooked chicken, chopped
8 cups fresh kale, trimmed and chopped
1 large peeled and chopped carrot
1 small finely chopped onion
½ tbsp. minced garlic
Salt
Freshly ground black pepper
6 cups homemade chicken broth

Directions:
In a slow cooker, add all ingredients and stir to combine.

Set the slow cooker on Low. Cover and cook for about 6 hours. Serve while hot.

Meatballs Soup

SERVES
12

MINUTES
20

Nutritional info: Cal 281, protein 27.5 g, fat 14.7 g, carbs 8.9 g

Ingredients:
For Meatballs:
2 lbs. grass-fed lean ground beef
4 garlic cloves, minced
¼ cup fresh chopped parsley leaves
½ cup Parmesan cheese, grated
1 organic egg, beaten
1 teaspoon dried oregano, crushed
1 teaspoon dried rosemary, crushed
Sea salt
Freshly ground black pepper
2 tbsps. coconut oil

For Soup:
1 chopped celery stalk
1 small chopped onion
1 small carrot, peeled and chopped
1 large plum tomato, chopped finely

3 large zucchinis, spiralized with blade C
Sea salt
Freshly ground black pepper
7 cups homemade beef broth

Directions:
For meatballs in a large bowl, add all ingredients and mix until well-combined. Make small sized balls from the mixture.

In a large skillet, heat oil over medium-high heat. In batches, add meatballs and cook for about 4-5 minutes or until golden brown from all sides. Remove from the heat.

In a slow cooker, add celery, onion, carrots and tomato. Place zucchini noodles over vegetables and sprinkle with salt and black pepper. Place the broth over vegetables. Carefully, add meatballs to the slow cooker.

Set the slow cooker on Low. Cover and cook for about 6 hours. Serve while hot.

Zucchini & Spinach Soup

SERVES
6

MINUTES
15

Nutritional info: Cal 79, protein 4.9 g, fat 3.5 g, carbs 7.8 g

Ingredients:
1 tbsp. olive oil
1 chopped onion
1 celery stalk, chopped
1 large carrot, peeled and chopped
2 garlic cloves, minced
1 tsp. dried and crushed oregano
1 large chopped zucchini
2 chopped tomatoes
2 cups fresh and chopped spinach
4 cups homemade vegetable broth
Sea salt
Freshly ground black pepper

Directions:

Set the slow cooker on high. Add oil and heat it. Add onion, celery and carrot and sauté for about 3-4 minutes. Add garlic and thyme and sauté for about 1 minute. Add remaining ingredients and stir to combine.

Set the slow cooker on Low. Cover and cook for about 6-8 hours. Serve while hot.

Squash & Apple Soup

SERVES
6

MINUTES
15

Nutritional info: Cal 133, protein 3.7 g, fat 1.4 g, carbs 30 g

Ingredients:
6 cups butternut squash, peeled and chopped
2 medium Granny Smith apples, peeled, cored and chopped
1 large carrot, peeled and chopped
1 small white onion, chopped
1 garlic clove, minced
2 cups homemade chicken broth
1 tsp. dried oregano, crushed
1 tsp. dried thyme, crushed
1 cup unsweetened almond milk
Sea salt
Ground black pepper

Directions:

In a large slow cooker, add all ingredients except almond milk and stir to combine.

Set the slow cooker on Low. Cover and cook for about 6-8 hours.

Uncover and stir in the almond milk. Let the soup cool slightly. In a blender, add the soup in batches and pulse till smooth.

Serve immediately while hot.

Beef Soup

SERVES
8

MINUTES
15

Nutritional info: Cal 303, protein 22.7 g, fat 20.5 g, carbs 9 g

Ingredients:

1½ lbs. grass-fed beef, cut into bite sized pieces

2 garlic cloves, minced

1½ cups fresh tomatoes, chopped

2 cups homemade vegetable broth

2 cups unsweetened coconut milk

2 tbsps. Italian seasoning

1 tbsp. dried basil, crushed

Sea salt

Ground black pepper

Directions:

In a slow cooker, add all ingredients and mix well. Set the slow cooker on Low. Cover and cook for 8-10 hours.

Serve while hot.

Seafood Soup

SERVES
8

MINUTES
10

Nutritional info: Cal 362, protein 50.5 g, fat 10.9 g, carbs 13.3 g

Ingredients:
6 cups homemade chicken broth
3 tbsps. olive oil
1 medium onion, chopped
½ cup carrot, peeled and chopped
½ cup celery stalk, chopped
6 cups fresh spinach, chopped
1 cup fresh tomatoes, chopped finely
4 garlic cloves, minced
1 cup fresh parsley, chopped
2 lbs. mussels, cleaned and debearded
2 lbs. sea scallops
1 lb. large shrimps, peeled and deveined
3 tbsps. fresh lime juice
Sea salt
Ground black pepper

Directions:

In a large slow cooker, add broth, oil, vegetables and parsley and mix.

Set the slow cooker on high. Cover and cook for 1¾ hours.

Uncover the slow cooker. Place mussels over vegetable mixture, followed by scallops and shrimp. Add lime juice and seasoning.

Cover and cook for about 35-45 minutes. Serve warm.

Coconut Pumpkin Soup

SERVES
6

MINUTES
10

Nutritional info: Cal 234, protein 2.3 g, fat 21.7 g, carbs 11.4 g

Ingredients:
1 diced onion
1 tsp. crushed ginger
1 tsp. crushed garlic
½ stick butter
1 pound pumpkin chunks
2 cups vegetable stock
1 2/3 cups coconut cream
Sea salt
Ground black pepper

Directions:
Combine all the ingredients in a slow cooker.
Cook for 4-6 hours on high.
Using an immersion blender puree the soup.
Serve while hot.

Creamy Beef Soup

SERVES
8

MINUTES
20

Nutritional info: Cal 536, protein 36.6 g, fat 40 g, carbs 7.1 g

Ingredients:
3 tbsps. butter
1 medium onion, chopped
2 celery stalks, chopped
2 large cloves garlic, minced
1 lb. grass-fed cooked beef, chopped
5 cups homemade beef broth
2 cups heavy cream
1½ cup shredded Swiss cheese
Sea salt
Ground black pepper

Directions:
In a skillet, melt butter on medium heat. Add onion, celery and garlic and sauté for about 5 minutes. Transfer the mixture into a slow cooker. Add beef, broth, salt and black pepper and stir to combine.

Set the slow cooker on High. Cover and cook for 4½ hours.
Uncover and stir in heavy cream and cheese. Cover and cook on high for about 1 hour.

Serve while hot.

KETOGENIC
POULTRY AND FISH BRUNCH RECIPES

Shredded Chicken and Bacon

SERVES
5

MINUTES
10

Nutritional info: Cal 545, protein 47.1 g, fat 38.8 g, carbs 1.9 g

Ingredients:

10 bacon slices

5 chicken breasts

2 tbsps. thyme, dried

1 tbsp. oregano, dried

1 tbsp. rosemary, dried

1 tbsp. salt

8 tbsps. olive oil

Directions:

Place all of the above ingredients in the slow cooker. Use 5 tablespoons of olive oil and mix together.

Cover and cook for about 8 hours on low.

When cooked, shred the meat. Mix with the remaining 3 tablespoons olive oil.

Creamy Mexican Chicken

SERVES
6

MINUTES
5

Nutritional info: Cal 262, protein 32 g, fat 13 g, carbs 10.5 g

Ingredients:
1 cup of sour cream
½ cup of chicken stock
14 oz. diced tomatoes and green chilies
1 batch of homemade taco seasoning
2 pounds chicken breast

Directions:
Place all of the above ingredients in the slow cooker. Mix together.

Cover and cook for about 6 hours on low. Serve.

Balsamic Chicken

SERVES
10

MINUTES
10

Nutritional info: Cal 190, protein 26 g, fat 6 g, carbs 5 g

Ingredients:
6 chicken breasts, skinless and boneless
14.5 oz. diced tomatoes
1 onion, thinly sliced
4 garlic cloves
½ cup balsamic vinegar
1 tbsp. olive oil
1 tsp. oregano, dried
1 tsp. rosemary, dried
1 tsp. basil, dried
½ tsp. thyme
Ground black pepper
Salt

Directions:
Place all of the above ingredients in the slow cooker. Mix together.
Cover and cook for about 4 hours on high.

Buffalo Chicken

SERVES
6

MINUTES
5

Nutritional info: Cal 297, protein 52 g, fat 8 g, carbs 1 g

Ingredients:
6 frozen chicken breasts
1 bottle of Franks Red hot
½ packet Hidden Valley ranch
3 tbsps. butter

Directions:
Place all of the above ingredients except butter in the slow cooker. Mix together.

Cover and cook for about 6 hours on low.

When cooked, shred the chicken. Mix with the 3 tablespoons butter.

Cook uncovered for another hour on low.

Coconut Chicken Curry

SERVES
6

MINUTES
10

Nutritional info: Cal 347, protein 29.2 g, fat 21.9 g, carbs 9.5 g

Ingredients:
1 pound cubed chicken
2 tbsps. curry paste
1 finely sliced onion
14 ounces pumpkin, cubed
1 1/3 cups coconut cream
14 ounces fresh spinach, chopped
Cashews

Directions:
Place all of the above ingredients in the slow cooker except the spinach and cashews. Mix together.

Cover and cook for about 6 hours on high.

Add the spinach 10 minutes prior serving and stir well. Serve the curry garnished with cashews.

Cheesy Tomato Chicken

SERVES
8

MINUTES
5

Nutritional info: Cal 349, protein 37.3 g, fat 17.4 g, carbs 8 g

Ingredients:

2 pounds frozen chicken breast, boneless
1 ½ cups diced tomatoes
16 ounces salsa
8 ounces cream cheese

Directions:

Place the chicken, tomatoes and salsa in a slow cooker. Cook for 4-5 hours on high.

Add the cream cheese and cook for another 30 minutes. Stir mix the chicken.

Serve on cauliflower rice.

Spicy Chicken Drumsticks

SERVES
2

MINUTES
10

Nutritional info: Cal 209, protein 27g, fat 9 g, carbs 3 g

Ingredients:
4 skinned chicken drumsticks
½ cup bottled Picante sauce
2 tsps. bottled cayenne pepper sauce
½ tsp. smoked paprika
1 bay leaf
¼ tsp. dried thyme
2 tsp. olive oil

Directions:
Place all of the above ingredients in the greased slow cooker. Mix together.

Cover and cook for about 6 hours on low.

Etouffee

SERVES
9

MINUTES
20

Nutritional info: Cal 247, protein 19 g, fat 1.3 g, carbs 6.2 g

Ingredients:
1 ½ pounds peeled and deveined raw shrimp
1 ½ pounds scallops, quartered
4 tablespoon olive oil
2 medium diced onions
9 rinsed and chopped scallions
3 diced celery stalks
2 small seeded and diced green bell peppers
2 small seeded and diced jalapeno peppers
3 cloves garlic, minced
20 ounces tomatoes, diced
5 tablespoons tomato paste
¾ teaspoon dried basil
¾ teaspoon dried thyme
¾ teaspoon dried oregano
1/3 teaspoon cayenne pepper
3 teaspoon almond meal
1 ½ tablespoons cold water

Hot sauce
Sea salt

Directions:
Combine the olive oil and onion in the slow cooker. Add the scallions, bell pepper, jalapeno, and celery. Mix well.

Cover and cook for 30 minutes on high.

Add the tomato paste and garlic. Cover and cook for 15 minutes on high.

Add the tomatoes, cayenne, thyme, oregano, basil, and salt. Set heat to low, cover, and cook for 6 hours.

Add the shrimp and scallops. Set heat to high, cover, and cook for 15 minutes.

Combine the almond meal and water. Mix well, then stir into the mixture in the slow cooker for about 6 minutes to thicken. Add a few drops of hot sauce and stir.

Poached Salmon

SERVES
8

MINUTES
15

Nutritional info: Cal 100, protein 40.1 g, fat 3.4 g, carbs 3.75 g

Ingredients:
2 tablespoons butter
1 large sweet onion, sliced into 8 rings
3 cups water
2 tablespoons lemon juice
2 sprigs fresh dill
8 salmon fillets, each of them weighs 6 oz. each
Sea salt
2 lemons, quartered

Directions:
Grease the inside of the slow cooker with the butter. Place the onion rings on the bottom in a single layer.

Slowly pour the water into the slow cooker. Cover and cook for half an hour on high.

Place the salmon fillets on top of the onion slices. Season with the fresh dill, salt, and some lemon juice.

Cover and cook for half an hour on high or until the salmon is no longer pink on the outside.

Drain the fillets very well and serve with the lemon wedges.

Chicken Fricassee

SERVES
9

MINUTES
20

Nutritional info: Cal 187, protein 31.6 g, fat 8.2 g, carbs 4 g

Ingredients:
6 cups leafy greens (bok choy, or collard greens)
2 thinly sliced carrots
2 diced celery stalks
5 chicken breasts, bone in, free range
1 cup chicken broth
3 teaspoons dried thyme
3 teaspoons dried parsley
3 teaspoons paprika

Directions:
Combine the carrot, celery, onion, and leafy greens in the slow cooker.

Place the chicken with the skin side facing up over the carrot mixture. Add the broth and sprinkle in the thyme, parsley, and paprika.

Cover and cook for 6 hours on low. Remove the skin before serving.

Chicken Stew

SERVES
6

MINUTES
15

Nutritional info: Cal 112, protein 14.9 g, fat 2.5 g, carbs 7 g

Ingredients:
3 (4 oz.) grass-fed boneless chicken breast, cubed
3 cups peeled and cubed carrots
½ cup chopped onions
2 garlic cloves, minced
Salt
Freshly ground black pepper
½ teaspoon dried and crushed thyme
2 cups homemade chicken broth

Directions:
In a large slow cooker, add all ingredients and stir to combine.

Set the slow cooker on low. Cover and cook for about 6 hours.
Serve while hot.

Salmon Stew

SERVES
4

MINUTES
10

Nutritional info: Cal 223, protein 24.7 g, fat 11 g, carbs 7.9 g

Ingredients:
1 lb. salmon fillet, cubed
1 tbsp. coconut oil
1 medium onion, chopped
1 garlic clove, minced
1 sliced zucchini
1 seeded and cubed green bell pepper
½ cup chopped tomatoes
1 cup homemade fish broth
¼ tsp. dried and crushed oregano
¼ tsp. dried and crushed basil
Salt
Freshly ground black pepper

Directions:
In a large slow cooker, add all ingredients and stir to combine.

Set the slow cooker on high. Cover and cook for about 6 hours.

Serve while hot.

Sicilian Tomato-braised Tuna

SERVES
4

MINUTES
10

Nutritional info: Cal 155, protein 41.1 g, fat 16.5 g, carbs 8 g

Ingredients:
2 tuna fillets (3 pounds)
½ cup olive oil
1 small red onion, chopped
6 cloves garlic, minced
3 cups gluten free, sugar-free tomato sauce
1 cup dry white wine
6 tablespoons drained and rinsed capers
4 tablespoons chopped fresh parsley
2 bay leaves
Sea salt
Freshly ground black pepper

Directions:

Place the tuna in a bowl of cold salted water to soak for about 12 minutes. Drain well and pat dry using paper towels.

Place a skillet over medium high flame and heat 2 tablespoons of oil. Sauté the onion and garlic until the onion is translucent. Transfer into the slow cooker.

Stir the wine, tomato, or marinara sauce, capers, bay leaves, and parsley into the slow cooker. Cover and cook for 1 hour on high.

Place the skillet over medium high heat and heat the rest of the oil. Brown the tuna fillets all over, then place into the slow cooker.

Cover and cook for 1 hour and 30 minutes on high, or until the tuna is cooked.

Take out the bay leaf and adjust the seasonings, if needed.

KETOGENIC
PORK, BEEF AND LAMB RECIPES

Oriental Braised Pork

SERVES
8

MINUTES
15

Nutritional info: Cal 454, protein 25.6 g, fat 3.4 g, carbs 3.75 g

Ingredients:

3 pounds of pastured pork loin

2 tablespoon red pepper flakes

4 cloves minced garlic

2 small minced onions

2 tsp garlic, ground

2 tsp ginger, ground

1 teaspoon cinnamon

1 tsp star anise, ground

2 tablespoon rice vinegar

6 tablespoon tamari soy sauce

2 teaspoon sesame oil

Directions:

Place a nonstick skillet over medium flame and brown the pork loin all over. Drain it well and transfer into the slow cooker.

Add the rest of the ingredients into the slow cooker.

Cover and cook for 8 hours on low. Serve warm.

Lamb Stew

SERVES
10

MINUTES
20

Nutritional info: Cal 388, protein 22.5 g, fat 19.5 g, carbs 10.1 g

Ingredients:
¼ cup olive oil, divided
2½ lbs. grass-fed lean stewed lamb, trimmed and cubed
Salt
Freshly ground black pepper
2 small chopped onions
1 tsp. dried thyme, crushed
1 tsp. dried oregano, crushed
1 tsp. dried basil, crushed
½ cup peeled and chopped carrot
1 celery stalk, chopped
10 cups trimmed and chopped fresh kale
1 cup finely chopped fresh tomatoes
2 cups homemade chicken broth
3 tbsps. fresh lemon juice

Directions:

In a large skillet, heat 2 tablespoons of butter on medium-high heat. Add lamb and sprinkle with salt and black pepper. Cook for about 4-5 minutes. Transfer the lamb into a large slow cooker.

In the same skillet, heat remaining oil. Add onions and sauté for about 4-5 minutes.

Transfer the onion mixture into the slow cooker. Add remaining ingredients except lemon juice and stir to combine.

Set the slow cooker on low. Cook for about 6 hours.

Uncover the slow cooker. With a slotted spoon, skim off the fats from the top.

Serve while hot with the drizzling of lemon juice.

Penang Beef Curry

SERVES
8

MINUTES
15

Nutritional info: Cal 256, protein 29 g, fat 14 g, carbs 2 g

Ingredients:

1 lb. beef, cubed

1 cup coconut cream

1 chopped onion

1 tsp. ground cardamom

1 tsp. Chinese five-spice

½ tsp. chili powder

1 tsp. ground cumin

1 tsp. turmeric

4 cloves

2 tsps. coriander

½ tsp. salt

Directions:

Put the coconut cream and all the spices into the slow cooker. Mix until well combined.

Add the chopped onion and cubed beef.

Cook for about 8–9 hours on low.

Top with some fresh coriander. Serve warm.

Mongolian Beef

SERVES
12

MINUTES
20

Nutritional info: Cal 370, protein 36.6 g, fat 11.9 g, carbs 4.75 g

Ingredients:

4 ½ pounds lean beef bottom roast, excess fat trimmed, grass fed

1 ½ knobs fresh ginger, peeled and grated

5 cloves garlic, grated

3 small onions, sliced thinly

2/3 cup water

2/3 cup coconut aminos

3 tablespoons hoisin sauce

3 tablespoons black vinegar

1 ½ tablespoons almond meal

1 ½ tablespoons five spice powder

1 ½ teaspoons red pepper flakes

1 ½ teaspoons sesame oil

Directions:

Combine the wet ingredients into the slow cooker. Add the ginger, garlic, onion, almond meal, five spice powder, and pepper flakes. Mix very well.

Add the roast and turn several times to coat. Cover and cook on low for 5 hours.

Slice the beef very thinly, then put the slices back into the slow cooker. Turn several times to coat in the sauce.

Cover and cook on high for 20 minutes. Serve warm.

Balsamic Glazed Short Ribs

SERVES
2

MINUTES
10

Nutritional info: Cal 410, protein 56.5 g, fat 42 g, carbs 7 g

Ingredients:
1 tbsp. olive oil
1 tsp. ground rosemary
4 beef short ribs
¼ cup balsamic vinegar
2 cloves garlic
½ cup dry red wine
Coconut oil
Black Pepper
Salt

Directions:
Season the beef with pepper and salt. In a skillet, cook beef in coconut oil over medium-high heat until all sides are brown.

Once done, place beef in the slow cooker along with the remaining ingredients. Cover and set on low.

Cook for about 6 hours. Serve warm.

Ropa Vieja

SERVES
6

MINUTES
10

Nutritional info: Cal 303, protein 24.5 g, fat 9.7 g, carbs 5 g

Ingredients:
1 ½ pounds lean flank steak
¼ tsp. salt
1 green pepper
3 tbsps. tomato paste
1 yellow pepper
¾ cup beef broth
1 onion, thinly sliced
¾ tsp. oregano
4 cloves garlic, minced
¾ tsp. cumin
1 bay leaf
Non-stick cooking spray

Directions:
Cover a slow cooker with non-stick cooking spray.

Remove the fat from the flank steak and place it in the slow cooker along with the remaining ingredients.

Set on low and cook for about 8 hours. Serve warm.

Lamb with Green Beans and Mint

SERVES
4

MINUTES
10

Nutritional info: Cal 286, protein 35.8 g, fat 21.3 g, carbs 16 g

Ingredients:

1.5 pounds lamb leg, boneless

½ tsp. salt

¼ cup fresh mint, chopped

2 tbsps. ghee

6 cups green beans, trimmed

4 cloves garlic, sliced

Ground black pepper

Directions:

Rub the lamb with pepper and salt. In a medium skillet, cook lamb in ghee until brown on all sides.

Transfer the meat into a slow cooker and distribute mint and garlic evenly.

Put a lid on the slow cooker and set it on high. Cook for 4 hours.

Remove the lamb temporarily from the slow cooker and put it in a plate.

Place the green beans in the bottom of the slow cooker and place the cooked lamb on top of it.

Continue cooking on high for 2 hours. Serve warm garnished with mint.

Lamb Curry

SERVES
6

MINUTES
10

Nutritional info: Cal 158, protein 20.3 g, fat 6.3 g, carbs 3.9 g

Ingredients:
1 sliced red onion
2 garlic cloves, crushed
2 tbsps. ground ginger
6 whole cloves
2 tsp. ground coriander
1 tsp. turmeric powder
½ tsp. chili powder
1 tsp. garam masala powder
2 tsp. ground cumin
1.1 pounds lamb, cubed
1.1 pounds frozen spinach (defrosted, water squeezed out)
14 ounces canned tomatoes, chopped.

Directions:
Combine all the ingredients in the slow cooker.

Cook for 4-5 hours on low. Serve warm.

Beef Arm Pot Roast

SERVES
6

MINUTES
10

Nutritional info: Cal 234, protein 33.1 g, fat 10.3 g, carbs 2.4 g

Ingredients:
2 pounds beef arm roast (trim any excess fat)
1 ½ tsps. sea salt
¾ tsp. ground black pepper
¾ tsp. finely chopped fresh basil
½ cup finely chopped yellow onion
4 minced garlic cloves
2 bay leaves
2 cups beef stock

Directions:
Season all sides of the roast with basil, salt and pepper.

Put in the slow cooker and add in the rest of the ingredients.

Cook for 8-10 hours on low.

Discard the bay leaves and slice the roast. Serve warm.

Lamb Roast

SERVES
6

MINUTES
10

Nutritional info: Cal 414, protein 26.7 g, fat 35.2 g, carbs 0.3 g

Ingredients:
2 pounds of lamb leg
¼ cup olive oil
2 tbsps. whole grain mustard
1 tbsp. maple syrup
4 thyme sprigs
6 mint leaves
¾ tsp. dried rosemary
¾ tsp. garlic
Salt
Black pepper

Directions:
Coat the lamb with the oil, maple syrup, mustard, rosemary, garlic, salt and pepper.

Place the lamb in the slow cooker.

104

Cook for 7 hours on low.

Throw in the mint and thyme and cook for another hour. Serve warm.

Pork Carnitas

SERVES
15

MINUTES
16

Nutritional info: Cal 265, protein 8 g, fat 9 g, carbs 0 g

Ingredients:
8 pounds Boston pork butt
2 tbsp. bacon grease
1 chopped onion
2 tbsps. cumin
2 tbsps. thyme
2 tbsps. chili powder
1 tbsp. salt
1 tbsp. ground black pepper
4 tbsps. minced garlic
1 cup water

Directions:
Add the bacon grease to the slow cooker and add in the onions and garlic.

Discard the fat off the meat and make a crisscross pattern on it.

Mix the spices together and rub it on the pork.

Add the pork to the slow cooker with a cup of water.

Cook for 8 hours on high. Serve warm.

KETOGENIC
VEGETARIAN AND VEGAN RECIPES

Green Artichoke Dip

SERVES
20

MINUTES
10

Nutritional info: Cal 83, protein 6.5 g, fat 8.3 g, carbs 3.6 g

Ingredients:
3 garlic cloves
½ medium onion
2 cans (14 ounces) artichoke hearts
10 ounces chopped spinach
10 ounces chopped kale
1 cup Parmesan cheese
1 cup shredded mozzarella cheese
1 cup Greek yogurt
¾ sour cream
¼ cup mayo
Salt
Pepper

Directions:
Place the artichokes, garlic and onion in a food processor and chop finely.

Transfer into a slow cooker with the rest of the ingredients.

Cook for 4 hours on high. Stir mix well, forming a paste. Serve with veggie sticks.

Summer Bruschetta

SERVES
4

MINUTES
15

Nutritional info: Cal 152, protein 0.4 g, fat 13 g, carbs 7.5 g

Ingredients:

6 chopped basil leaves
½ cup artichoke hearts, quartered
¼ cup halved Kalamata olives
¼ cup capers
20 diced Roma tomatoes
3 tbsps. balsamic vinegar
3 tbsps. avocado oil
¾ tsp. onion powder
¾ tsp. sea salt
½ tsp. black pepper
2 tbsps. minced garlic

Directions:

Combine all the ingredients in the slow cooker and mix well.

Cook for 3 hours on high, stirring the mix after every hour.

Italian Style Mushrooms

SERVES
6

MINUTES
10

Nutritional info: Cal 99, protein 3 g, fat 8 g, carbs 6 g

Ingredients:
1 pound fresh mushrooms
1 sliced onion
½ cup melted butter
1 envelope Italian salad dressing mix

Directions:
Spread the mushrooms and onion in a slow cooker.

Whisk together the butter and dressing mix and pour over the mushrooms.

Cook covered for 4-5 hours on low.

Cheese Sauced Cauliflower & Broccoli

SERVES
10

MINUTES
15

Nutritional info: Cal 177, protein 8 g, fat 12 g, carbs 10 g

Ingredients:
4 cups broccoli florets
4 cups cauliflower florets
1 chopped onion
14 ounces Alfredo pasta sauce
6 ounces Swiss cheese, torn
1 tsp. dried thyme
¼ tsp. ground black pepper
½ cup ranch flavored sliced almonds

Directions:
Combine all the ingredients in a slow cooker except the almonds.

Cook covered for 6-7 hours on low.

Stir gently and serve garnished with almonds.

Pesto Mushrooms with Ricotta

SERVES
4

MINUTES
15

Nutritional info: Cal 400, protein 19 g, fat 34 g, carbs 2 g

Ingredients:
5 tbsps. extra virgin olive oil
16 chestnut mushrooms
8 ¾ ounces Ricotta
2 finely chopped garlic cloves
2 tbsps. basil pesto
1 ounce freshly grated Parmesan
2 tbsps. freshly chopped parsley
Extra Pesto

Directions:
Brush the mushrooms with oil and place in a slow cooker cap side down, in a single layer.

Mix together the rest of the ingredients except the oil and Parmesan.

Spoon the mixture into the mushrooms.

Sprinkle the Parmesan and remaining oil over the mushrooms.

Cook for 8-9 hours on low. Serve with extra pesto.

Creamy Spinach Curry

SERVES
8

MINUTES
10

Nutritional info: Cal 91, protein 4 g, fat 6 g, carbs 3 g

Ingredients:
3 packages (10 ounces) frozen spinach (thawed)
1 chopped onion
4 minced garlic cloves
2 tbsps. curry powder
2 tbsps. melted butter
½ cup vegetable stock
¼ cup heavy cream
1 tsp. lemon juice

Directions:
Dump all ingredients in a crock pot except the cream and lemon juice.

Cook covered for 3-4 hours on low.

Mix in the lemon juice and cream, 30 minutes prior to the completion of cook time and cook covered. Serve warm.

Herbed Garlic Mushrooms

SERVES
4

MINUTES
10

Nutritional info: Cal 120, protein 6 g, fat 8 g, carbs 7 g

Ingredients:
24 ounces cremini mushrooms
4 minced garlic cloves
½ tsp. basil, dried
½ tsp. oregano, dried
¼ tsp. dried thyme
2 bay leaves
1 cup vegetable broth
¼ cup Half-and-half
2 tbsps. unsalted butter
2 tbsps. freshly chopped parsley leaves
Kosher sea salt
Black pepper

Directions:

Combine all the ingredients except the butter, half and half and fresh parsley in a slow cooker.

Cook covered for 3-4 hours on low.

20 minutes prior to the completion of cook time, mix in the butter and half-and-half.

Garnish with parsley and serve.

Zucchini Lasagna

SERVES
8

MINUTES
20

Nutritional info: Cal 251, protein 20.8 g, fat 13.9 g, carbs 11.9 g

Ingredients:
4 sliced zucchini
4 cups of homemade tomato sauce
15 ounces ricotta cheese
1 large egg
¼ cup freshly grated Parmesan cheese
1 cup chopped spinach
Salt
Pepper
16 ounces shredded mozzarella
2 tsps. freshly chopped parsley

Directions:
Mix together the spinach, egg, ricotta cheese and half the Parmesan cheese in a bowl.

Spread a cup of tomato sauce in a greased slow cooker and spread 5 zucchini slices over it, slightly overlapping.

Spread some of the egg mixture over and sprinkle some Mozzarella.

Repeat the layering until all the ingredients are used up, topping with Parmesan cheese and Mozzarella.

Cook covered for 3½ - 4 hours on high. Serve garnished with parsley.

Cheesy Broccoli

SERVES
10

MINUTES
10

Nutritional info: Cal 104, protein 7.2 g, fat 4.9 g, carbs 9.7 g

Ingredients:
8 cups broccoli florets
1 large onion, chopped
1 tablespoon fresh rosemary, minced
1½ cups Swiss cheese, grated
1¾ cups homemade tomato sauce
1 tbsp. fresh lemon juice
Sea salt and freshly ground black pepper

Directions:
In a large slow cooker, place all ingredients and mix well.

Set the slow cooker on Low. Cover and cook for about 6-7 hours. Serve hot.

Veggie Casserole

SERVES
10

MINUTES
15

Nutritional info: Cal 89, protein 5.7 g, fat 4.5 g, carbs 8 g

Ingredients:
1 tbsp. unsalted butter, melted
4 medium zucchinis, peeled and sliced
1 green bell pepper, seeded and sliced
2 cups finely chopped fresh tomatoes
1 thinly sliced white onion
1 tbsp. fresh thyme, minced
½ cup grated Parmesan cheese
Sea salt
Freshly ground black pepper

Directions:
In a large slow cooker, place all ingredients except cheese and mix well.

Set the slow cooker on low. Cover and cook for about 3 hours.

Uncover and sprinkle with cheese evenly. Cover and cook for about 1½ hours.

Serve hot.

Printed in Great Britain
by Amazon